The Mystery *of* LOVE

CARDINAL BASIL HUME

PARACLETE PRESS

BREWSTER, MASSACHUSETTS

Library of Congress Cataloging-in-Publication Data

Hume, Basil, 1923-1999
  The mystery of love / Basil Hume.
    p. cm.
  Originally published: London : Darton, Longman and Todd, 2000.
  ISBN 1-55725-280-7 (pbk.)
    1. Spiritual life—Catholic Church. 2. Love—Religious aspects—
Catholic Church. 3. Catholic Church—Doctrines. I. Title.

  BX2350.3 .H85 2001   2001003225
  248.4'82—dc21

10 9 8 7 6 5 4 3 2 1

First published in Great Britain in 1996 by Hodder & Stoughton
Published in Great Britain in 2000 by Darton,
Longman and Todd Ltd
© 1976, 1995, 1996 and 2000 Cardinal Basil Hume

This edition published by Paraclete Press, 2001
ISBN 1-55725-280-7

Brewster, Massachusetts
www.paracletepress.com

Printed in the United States of America.

We need heralds of the Gospel
who are experts in humanity,
who know the depths of the human heart,
who can share the joys, the hopes,
the agonies, the distress of people today,
but who are, at the same time,
contemplatives who have fallen in love with
God.

Pope John Paul II

Modern man listens more readily
to witnesses than to teachers,
and if he listens to teachers
it is because they are witnesses.

Pope Paul VI

Contents

Foreword

FOR THE FIRST SIX YEARS OF HIS TIME in Westminster I had the joy of being private secretary to Cardinal Hume. They were his salad days as he settled into a new ministry on a national scale. Though his previous role as Abbot of Ampleforth had been a good noviciate in many ways, nevertheless the leap in responsi bility was on the quantum scale. In a pressurised and intensely public position the Cardinal found great solace in his pastoral visits around the parishes of his large archdiocese. He would arrive in the appointed church in time for the evening Mass and then after-wards mingle with the congregation in the parish hall. It was a simple yet intensely satisfying routine, both for himself and the parish in question. From 1976 until 1982 I must have heard virtually every homily Cardinal Hume preached around the diocese. They were good nourishment for the spirit and many snippets from those original homilies pop up in the following pages.

Originally these "points for meditation" appeared in a privately produced edition arranged by Heather

Craufurd. It was the Cardinal's intention that in time a hardback edition of those reflections should appear, thus enabling it to be a kind of prayer book. He wanted the extracts to be used as "starting points for prayer and meditation." From his new vantage point he will be pleased that this hope has now been fulfilled.

He will be glad too that due credit is given to Heather Craufurd. There is a nice story attached to her involvement with the Cardinal's publications. It fell to me in those early days in Westminster to make the introductions. Heather had begun typing the Cardinal's homilies when ever he was within striking distance of her London home. She turned up one day at Archbishop's House to meet me with the request that she be allowed to continue with this enriching pastime. Thus it was that her apostolate gathered pace, and with it plenty of material, as the years passed. In his Foreword to the original private production Cardinal Hume paid tribute to Heather's support in his writing ministry. His debt to her is considerable because he prized the opportunity this gave him to share the things of God with a larger audience than would other wise have been possible.

In his last few days on earth the Cardinal shared with me a meditation on the Our Father. It was, he said, like discovering its meaning for the very first time:

"It's only now that I begin to glimpse how everything we need is contained right there in the Lord's own prayer." He then prayed the opening three sentences of the Our Father, adding each time a tiny commentary of his own:

**Our Father who art in heaven hallowed
be Thy name:**
to sing the praises of God,
it is for that for which we were made,
and it is that which will be for all eternity,
our greatest joy.

Thy Kingdom come:
the Gospel values of Jesus—justice, love,
and peace—embraced throughout the world and in
all their fullness.

Thy will be done on earth as it is in heaven:
that is the only thing which really matters.
What God wants for us
is what is best for us.

The poignant context gives an especially luminous quality to these particular words, but everything here is likely to provide a trigger for prayer. How happy he will be to know that what follows will help us in raising our minds and hearts to God.

Rt. Rev. John Crowley
Bishop of Middlesbrough

Mystery

THE MEANING OF THINGS and their purpose is, in part, now hidden, but it will in the end become clear. The choice is between the mystery and the absurd.

To embrace the mystery is to discover the real. It is to walk towards the light, to glimpse the morning star, to catch sight from time to time of what is truly real. It is no more than a flicker of light through the cloud of unknowing: a fitful ray of light that is a messenger from the sun which is hidden from your gaze.

You see the light but not the sun. When you set yourself to look more closely, you will begin to see some sense in the darkness that surrounds you. Your eyes will begin to pick out the shape of things and persons around you. You will begin to see in them the presence of the One who gives them meaning and purpose, and that it is he who is the explanation of them all.

The mysteries which we have been given to reflect upon, and make part of our lives, are so much greater, so much bigger, so much beyond our capacity to understand. Our minds are so small, so terribly small, that we are always at the foothills in our understanding of God and his world. But I think that is good, because eventually, when we get to the top, we will then see the full vision.

A mystery is a reality which we can never understand, nor even discover for ourselves. This mystery can never be solved. It can only be entered and explored by one who accepts with awe and reverence that the deepest reality is un-imaginably greater than we can ever comprehend; that beyond the limitations of our senses, and even the horizon of death, lies a place of inexpressible joy, the fountain of all life and love.

❧

We talk about the Sacred Mysteries. It is a word used in the New Testament, a word which has been used by Christian writers all down the ages and quite especially in relation to the Sacraments. So when I use the word mystery I mean a divine reality which we could never discover for ourselves, and can only ever understand very, very inadequately. Mysteries are truths revealed by God which we, in our prayer and practice throughout life, explore and try to understand just a little bit more. It is a lovely word—mystery.

❧

There is an ancient story about St. Augustine, theologian and great Father of the Church. It relates how one day, walking along the beach, he saw a small boy who, having dug a hole in the sand, was running to and from the sea pouring water into it with his shell. Asked what he was doing he answered: "I'm going to put the whole ocean into this hole." When told that was impossible he replied: "'It is easier to put the whole ocean into this hole than for you to under stand the Mystery of the Trinity." That story is applicable to all the great Mysteries of our Faith.

The Life in the Spirit is the only authentic means of responding to the mystery of ourselves and of our existence. It is not therefore the preserve of the religious elite. It is a treasure to be found in the midst of daily life, in the home and family, in all the activities of a busy fulfilled life, in the pain and desolation of bereavement, sickness, handicap, and loneliness. In all the circumstance of our lives we can find God, experience his healing and presence, and that joy and peace which the world cannot give.

Shafts of light

It is as if a cloud hovers between us and God. From time to time that cloud of unknowing is pierced by a shaft of light which tells us some thing about God, though we do not see or touch him directly.

It may be a moment of total happiness, an experience of true love, a discovery of the secrets locked away in the universe. Conversely, it may be in sorrow and sadness that we experience his presence. In ecstasies and agonies his voice is unmistakable to those prepared to listen and look.

"Man is made in the image and likeness of God." Every person with whom I come into contact is not only going to tell me something of God, but is also going to reveal something of God's love for me. I like to think that the affection another shows to me is a special word of love from God. It is as if every person who shows affection for me is in some way transmitting God's love to me.

The purpose of life

What is the purpose of life? The search for meaning and the desire for happiness are basic drives within the human psyche, and they are strong and deep. It is the mind seeking its object, which is *truth*; it is the will wanting its object, the *good*.

Truth and goodness in their absolute forms are found in God alone. The awareness of them, as far as it is possible in our present state, is a glimpse of his glory which is beauty in its purest form. To know truth, to love goodness, to delight in beauty, this is our human purpose or—more simply—to know God, to love him, and to praise him.

The desire for happiness

We naturally and instinctively recoil from those things that threaten, or deprive us of, our happiness; from pain and suffering, for example. We naturally want, and reach out for, those things that give us contentment, well-being, or fulfilment. Experience teaches us that it is not easy to find those things that will give us what we are looking for. Of course we can and do find happiness now, but it is never quite complete, and it does not last. All human activity is ultimately related to our search, wittingly or unwittingly, for total truth and total happiness—which is God. Our searching is, in fact, only in response to an initiative which comes from elsewhere: We would not be seeking God, unless he were first seeking us. He wants us to find him; he is on our side. In the depths of our being he is drawing us to seek him ever more overtly, more persistently, as life goes on.

Of one thing I am convinced; the search has a happy ending. Our desires have an achievable goal for all of us, total union with God.

Faith

IF YOU REALLY GET TO THINK DEEPLY about the things of God, then you come very soon to a level beyond which the human mind cannot go.

You can go so far paddling in the sea, and there comes a point where it has to carry you. So it is that reason can only go so far, and then comes the point where faith has to carry you.

So you get very quickly to mystery, and mystery is defined, by me anyway, as a secret reality about God which lies beyond our capacity either to discover or to understand.

Faith and doubt

Doubt is the instrument to purify my faith. It is only when I begin to doubt that I really make an honest act of faith:

Lord, I do believe; help thou my unbelief.

Time and again it is against all the odds, against everything my brain is telling me. But faith must be purified time and again, because it is the purification of faith that leads to growth in love.

That perfect act of faith, which is always made in pain and sometimes in agony, leads in a most remarkable way to peace and serenity. Why? Because faith is a gift of God.

"Who do men say that I am?" When Our Lord put this question to St. Peter, he answered with the faith of the whole early Church and every generation since: "Thou art the Christ, the Son of the living God." Reflect on the place Jesus Christ has in your life and whether it affects your faith and helps you to believe and say, as did St. Thomas: "My Lord and my God."

We need in our day to affirm our faith in Jesus Christ, true God and true man, and there is another faith which follows from that: our faith in the presence of Christ in the Blessed Sacrament—Christ wholly present, body, soul, and divinity. Prayer to Our Lady can deepen our faith in Jesus Christ her Son and his presence in the Eucharist. Ask for that grace, because when we are touched in our faith in Christ and his presence in the Eucharist, that has an effect on the whole life of the Church, far beyond our own personal faith.

Sometimes I am uncertain, hesitant, when in a very Godless world I am tempted to doubt. Then I remember the words: "Would you, too, go away?" There is, I think, a note of anxiety in his voice, just in case we might. Of course we do not. "Lord, to whom should we go? Thy words are the words of eternal life; we have learned to believe and are assured that thou art the Christ, the Son of God." (John 6:69) That is often an act of faith made by you and by me when reason is of no avail, and there is only darkness around with no one to guide and help. It is the finest of prayers, for it is the desire to love the unseen which prompts it, not the evidence of our senses. It is one to which he listens readily, and rejoices when it is said.

The eyes of faith

One of my favorite places in Lourdes is the zigzag path down to the Grotto. What you see on the first corner is a statue of Bartimaeus, the blind man. Why is it there? Looking over the Grotto, he sees nothing because he is blind. That statue was placed there by an Italian who, though not cured of her blindness, rediscovered her faith, which she realized was more to be prized than physical sight.

> "What wouldst thou have me do for thee?"
> "Lord, that I may see." And Jesus said to him:
> "Go home; thy faith hath made thee whole."

Immediately he recovered his sight and followed Jesus. (Mark 10:46-52)

The point about that story is not that the blind man got back his physical sight, which indeed he did; the important point is that he followed Jesus.

What is important for us in following Jesus is that we should get back the inward eye, the inner light. So we pray, not for a physical miracle, but a spiritual change.

The inner life: that part of us where faith and doubt contest the mastery, and where alas, doubt prevails because it is the stronger of the two, though not the wiser. Without faith, life is emptied of its true meaning and purpose.

A long time ago I had a friend who had been born blind. He had one great enthusiasm in his life and that was watching cricket. He had no idea what cricket looked like. Yet he had this tremendous interest, almost a passion for it. I used to take him to matches, sit beside him, giving a running commentary. He would be riveted and get very excited.

The point is this: He was totally dependent on what I was saying to him. I could have been telling him a pack of lies. We might not even have been watching a cricket match at all. But, no, as I described the game, he got more and more interested and involved.

It was that experience that taught me about faith. Because I do not see God with my eyes, I do not see him present in the Blessed Sacrament. I did not see him rise from the dead. I have not seen any of these things with my eyes. I cannot touch God with my hands, nor hear his voice with my ears. So in a way we are all blind, like that man at the cricket match.

You and I depend entirely on what God tells us. That is why the Word of God is so important. Faith is listening to what God has to say through the Scriptures.

The difference between faith and theology

When I come into a church and see the little red light burning in front of the tabernacle, I genuflect. Why? It is my act of faith in the presence of Our Lord in the Blessed Sacrament. I do it because I believe that Christ is truly present there. I genuflect because of my faith. How do I believe? The brain begins to wonder, and that is theology. I don't believe because I have worked it out. But because I believe, I want to think about it, meditate on it. That is the difference between faith and the reason I use to examine my belief. But if I come into church and automatically and unthinkingly genuflect while still talking to someone, then I am not expressing my faith. The point is that external gestures express our faith and help to strengthen it. That is why signs and gestures are so important.

Very often people say they find it difficult to believe. What they are really saying is that they are finding it difficult to understand. Belief is one thing, understanding another. You do not believe because you understand. It is not because I have understood that I genuflect, it is because I believe what Our Lord said.

Our Blessed Lady

THE BIRTH OF MARY CONSTITUTED a new beginning for humanity. She was part of God's plan to put right the tragic result of sin in our own personal times and in our society as a whole. But sin never touched her, for she was conceived immaculate. She was born perfect, full of grace and surely gifted with all those human qualities which we instinctively admire: She was understanding, compassionate, affectionate, with a presence that inspired confidence in others weaker and more fragile than she. I believe that all who met her were immediately drawn to her. She had an attractive personality. People wanted to be with her.

Mother of God

The moment Our Lady had said her "Fiat"—let it be done—the moment she had given her agreement, she conceived and began to be with child. Just think of that and marvel. Life began in her at that moment:

new life, Christ's life, life that was uniquely sacred because it was his life. It was at that moment that she became, in fact, the Mother of God.

This simple and profound truth has still in our day much to say that is important and profound. She remained virgin because it was the power of the Holy Spirit that was at work within her. My mind, my reason can scarcely carry such truths. They lie way beyond my understanding and always will. I can do no more than say: "I believe." My acceptance of that great truth is a gift from God. It is the act of faith which is my assent, my "Fiat" to what the Church has taught down the ages. But my faith in what the Church has taught from earliest times has got to match her trust and her humility as she accepted what must have appeared, even to her, the unbelievable message of the angel that she was to be a mother. As with all acts of faith, it is moving into a level of understanding which lies beyond all our capacities and leads us into the secrets which are God's, and to wonder, marvel, and praise.

Mary, Mother of the Church

You recall that scene as Our Lord was dying on the cross when he turned to Our Blessed Lady saying, "Woman, behold thy son," then, turning to St. John, "Son, behold thy Mother." That was a precious and important moment because as Our Blessed Lady was standing at the foot of the cross agonizing with her

Son, she was, in a manner of speaking, experiencing birth pangs as the Church of God was coming to birth out of the pierced side of Christ. Water and blood flowed from it, symbolizing Baptism and the Eucharist: Baptism which makes us members of the Church, and the Eucharist that by which we live. Mary at that moment became Mother of the Church, our mother. So from earliest times it has been instinctive among Christians to turn to her for all our needs, and to recognize the part that she must play in the lives of each one of us.

Mary, our mother

We give to Our Lady all those lovely titles: Queen of Heaven, Queen of Angels, and, greatest of all titles, Mother of God. Awesome titles indeed. But then we remember that we also call her Refuge of Sinners, Help of Christians, Comforter of the Afflicted, because this great lady is our mother too. So, poor as we are, weak though we may be, in need of healing as we surely are, we kneel in prayer and ask for her help. Instinctively, we turn to Mary, Christ's mother and our mother.

Jesus was so anxious to give us his mother to be our mother. Why? Because mothers never reject us, or at least not normally, when we walk away or wander off, or just drift. Mothers are always there, waiting, wanting, loving. Mothers like that show us, as Mary does in a remarkable way, that there is in God motherhood as well as fatherhood. Mary, above all, gives us that important truth.

How desperately we need in our time the light of hope. We call upon Mary our mother to intercede so that there will be that increase of hope which comes from faith and leads to love.

Hope

HOPE COMES FROM FAITH and leads to love. It is, in part, a state of expectancy, the looking forward to the fulfilment of God's promises to us. In part it must be in God's goodness and love. These will sustain us when the going gets rough, or the way is difficult.

It is hope which spurs us on to risk all for the love of God. It is hope which gives rise to great enterprises undertaken for the honor and glory of God.

There is an urgent task to be done in our time. It is to give hope to a world where disillusionment is widespread to show our contemporaries that in the Word of God, and in his Sacraments, they can be touched by the divine and be cheered.

❧

We are not living in a world devoid of hope and divorced from God. We may be buffeted by the prevailing winds of unbelief. We may suffer from society's generalized distrust of organized religion and Church structures. But at the same time there is still to be found in unexpected places a persistent thirst for God and for the life of the Spirit, a certain longing for prayer and meditation, and a curiosity about all forms of religious experience. There remains the inner restlessness of the human spirit and its ceaseless search for meaning and fulfilment. Individuals are thus kept open to the possibility of God and receptive to the Spirit.

If we do not believe there is a heaven beyond and outside this present life, for which we are ultimately destined, then life is difficult indeed and our mood one of pessimism. Why? Man has deep aspirations and limitless desires which almost instinctively we sense must be fulfilled or else life is absurd and certain failure. No, it is not so. There is a gentle breeze, if we can but catch it, which blows all the time to help us on our journey through life to our final destination. That breeze is the Holy Spirit.

Life is often like going through a dark tunnel, knowing that at the end there is *light*. But you have to keep going. From time to time there are chinks of light, but you have to pass beyond them.

It is the memory of those chinks that keeps you going along the tunnel of life, knowing that at the end you will be coming out into this marvellous light. All the time, someone is walking with you, helping you, sometimes carrying you.

Hope is knowing that I have
been forgiven, my guilt removed.

Hope is knowing that there is a
future, a life after death.

Hope is knowing that there is love,
that there is a God,
and I am loved by him.
Whatever happens he *does* care.

Hope is knowing that he has plans,
even if I do not understand them.

The Mystery of Love

TOO OFTEN PEOPLE ARE BROUGHT UP with a wrong concept of God, and their reaction to him is one of fear or apprehension. This can take many years to break down. The simple thought that God loves me, and the words used to describe human love such as warmth, intensity, strong, unreserved, all have a meaning in describing God's love. It is quite literally true that no one can, or will ever, love me more than God does; nor will any experience of mine ever, even in the dimmest way, reflect God's love for me. There are no limits to God.

When we ponder on what the Gospel tells us of Our Lord, we cannot fail to be moved and reassured. In Luke, chapter 15, we see how enormously sensitive he was to tax collectors and sinners. Anyone who feels depressed and fears rejection by God should read quietly the whole of that chapter. There we read of the shepherd's concern for the one sheep out of a fold of a hundred which has strayed. The sheep may be lost in fog or wandering aimlessly, but the shepherd is always in search of it. No matter how desperate our plight, we may always rely on the love which will never tire of seeking us out.

Whatever may be the burden of sin or guilt we carry, God is always there waiting for us. He waits; he does not force.

※

Love is an art to be learned. It is a giving experience, a selfless act.

Every experience of love gives us yet another glimpse of the meaning of love in God himself. Human love is the instrument we can use to explore the mystery of love which God is.

※

We are, as we go through life, like lovers in search of the Beloved. That is the only way to try to understand our response to God's love for us. We are lovers in search of the Beloved, simply because he is in search of each one of us and sees each one as his Beloved.

Jesus had a human heart, an affectionate nature, and emotions like ours, never running wild or out of control as is sometimes the case with us. He knew the joys of human love and its pains. He loved Judas, but Judas was to betray him. That hurt.

Yes, Jesus loved in a human way. Indeed, no one loved more perfectly in a human way than he or knew better how to love as a friend. There was more, however, to Jesus' loving. His loving was an icon of his loving as God.

❧

Love was a reality in God long before it ever became an experience between humans. It has been well said that the language of love belongs by right first to God. If we want to know what love truly is, then we shall not do so until we see God in vision. Then we shall see it in all its beauty and truth. Human love reflects divine love and, indeed, transmits it.

Friendship with God

Holiness involves friendship with God. The movement towards the realization of God's love for us is similar to our relationship with other people. There comes a moment which we can never quite locate or catch, when an acquaintance becomes a friend. In a sense, the change from one to the other has been taking place over a period of time. But there comes a point when we know we can trust the other, exchange confidences, keep each other's secrets: We are friends. There has to be a moment like that in our relationship with God. He ceases to be just a Sunday acquaintance and becomes a weekday friend.

Forgiveness

When we love we want to forgive. It is so with God. Remember the tax gatherer (Luke 18) at the back of the Temple not daring to raise his eyes, in contrast to the Pharisee who prayed at the front, boasting of his accomplishments. It was not he who was justified, but the tax gatherer who prayed: "Lord, be merciful to me a sinner."

That is a most marvellous prayer. Who, praying that, can fail to hear in his or her heart those words of Our Lord on the cross: "Father, forgive them; they know not what they do."

It is beautiful to receive God's forgiveness, and it is there for the taking.

God the tremendous lover

Always think of God as your lover. Therefore he wants to be with you, just as a lover always wants to be with the beloved. He wants your attention, as every lover wants the attention of the beloved. He wants to listen to you, as every lover wants to hear the voice of the beloved. If you turn to me and ask, "Are you in love with God?" I would pause, hesitate and say, "I am not certain. But of one thing I *am* certain—that he is in love with me."

He wants also to whisper a word of love into my ear. It may be a word of forgiveness; it may be a word of healing; it may be a word of comfort; it may even be a word of rebuke. He speaks to us deep down. Isn't it sad if the beloved disappoints the lover through negligence, or through walking away through stupidity?

Two great qualities of God: his fidelity to us and his tenderness. I love that idea of God being faithful to me. However much I go wrong, however far I may stray, whatever follies I may engage in, he remains faithful to me.

※

In the person I love is the One I am seeking. If I find myself loving a person it is only because I am trying to find, in and beyond that person, the God who is Love.

In the person who loves me I discover the One who loves me most. Because I love, I experience from that other person just a little bit of the way God feels about me. In the person who attracts me is the God who is drawing me. When I find a person I love, I always take it as a message of God's love. The more you love, the more messages there are.

God's tutors

You may not be in love with God, but God is most certainly in love with you. Always remember that. He has given you two tutors who will give you your first lessons in mature religious response. They are called love and pain. It is love which will attach you to God, and pain will detach you from exclusive entanglement with the goods of this world. Once you begin to respond to these two tutors you will want to discover more about that God who is in love with you. You will then grow to appreciate what God has told us in the Scriptures, and what he gives us through the Sacraments.

He teaches me in the love I experience and the suffering I know, the latter to detach me from this world, the former a foretaste of that endless now of ecstatic love which is union with him. Then, our journey completed, a journey made with him who is the Way, the Truth, and the Life, happiness is achieved.

※

"Like an eagle that watches its nest, that hovers over its young . . ." (Deuteronomy 32:11). The image of the eagle watching over its nest is a beautiful one. The transcendence and majesty of God does not impose, does not smother us, but invites and beckons us to open our hearts and feed on his love. To hear the voice of God demands solitude, silence, and stillness. In our society today there is too much noise, both around and within us, and the quiet voice of God becomes stifled. But in a moment of gentle stillness God not only reveals something of himself, but transforms us too.

I thirst

When Our Lord said these words, there is no doubt that in that situation of intense suffering, he was in need of drink. But Our Lord was also in need of love. After all, the whole world had turned against him. He was being tortured, crucified, and insulted. Those are moments when we experience the need for love, to be wanted by, as well as to want, another.

Our Lord was expressing that need—God speaking through the humanity of Christ. That is an astonishing thought, God thirsting for me. Too many people doubt God's love for them.

> Kneel in prayer at the foot of the cross
> and let him whisper in your ear:
> I thirst,
> I thirst for you.

Is There a God?

IT IS VERY IMPORTANT TO BE ABLE TO SAY to people: "Yes, there is a God." You can only know God through what he says, or if somehow or other he could come down to our level, and he would have to do that in human terms. That is the Incarnation, God becoming man. But if you are talking to an atheist who says there is no God and you say "Yes, there is," the answer you will get is, "Prove it." It is no good saying to that person, "Jesus Christ was God." Nor can you say that you have had a great "light" inside yourself. So what do you point to? Well, there are four arguments and they are all different.

- The easiest one is to look at what God has done. What strikes us is the consistency we find in nature, the marvel that creation is, what people call harmony and order, the sheer wonder of the human body, the sheer wonder of the rhythm in nature. Learned people have said, "Because there is order in the world, then surely there must be a mind which is responsible."

- The second argument, which was used by Cardinal Newman, lies in the instinct we have which we call conscience. There are a lot of things where conscience tells us something is right or wrong. It is almost primeval. Even in a baby or a young child we can see in a simple way the working out of conscience.
- There is a third argument. It is when you look at certain values like goodness and beauty. Goodness and beauty must have come from that which is in itself good and in itself beautiful.
- The fourth argument is for me the best. It is the hardest to see, yet the most convincing. Everything that you and I know and experience depends on somebody or something else. All living creatures depend on the oxygen in the atmosphere. It is intellectually impossible to accept a world where everything depends on something else if there is not something outside the whole thing which is not dependent on something else. Things don't last for ever, they have a beginning and an end. They are contingent. If you think about that, then you see there must be a Being who is totally necessary for the beginning of everything else.

Those four arguments come from the rational, but there is an intuitive part—call it a gut feeling, inspiration, insight.

People reject things they do not understand. The trouble with contemporary science or philosophy is that they hold that what cannot be known through experiment does not exist. If I understood suffering, I would be God. When I had the terrible experience of witnessing the starving and dying in Ethiopia, one of the television crew came up to me and asked, "Doesn't this shake your belief in God?" I had to answer the question. After pausing I said, "No, not really, but I do not understand."

Abandonment to God's Will

"INTO THY HANDS, LORD, I COMMEND my spirit." The Word—this is Jesus Christ, true God and true man. The words he spoke are not constrained or limited by time or space. He spoke once but his word goes on echoing down the years like a voice echoing round the mountains. It is present, real, and actual now, as when it was first spoken. His last words have a special significance, the last words of a dying man.

Remember that struggle in the Garden of Gethsemane. Jesus was in agony. His prayer was: "Let this chalice pass from me, but let your will be done, not mine." He wanted to be freed from it, but he accepted the will of God. You know as well as I do what a difference there is between the penances we choose for ourselves, and those which we do not. The cross we are often asked to carry never fits our shoulders. Yet that is the one we are asked to carry.

❧

"Into thy hands . . ." The true import and significance of those words becomes even clearer when we remember the words he spoke just before: "My God, my God, why hast thou forsaken me?" All down the ages saints and mystics have wondered what it could mean. What was it that Our Lord was experiencing at that moment, quite apart from the anguish because of the acute suffering which crucifixion indeed was? There was that agony of mind which can surely be more terrible and more frightening than physical pain. Complete darkness, as I would think, in his human mind. We have, no doubt, all known persons who at some time in their lives have experienced that inner darkness; I think perhaps all of us at some time or other have experienced it to a greater or lesser degree.

Very often when people are dying, or are very sick, they go through darkness. They ask themselves whether it is all true, whether they are going into nothingness. Those are genuine trials which people experience, a sense of having been forsaken. I think it must be the most terrible of trials. I say this not to cause distress, but just so that if it does happen, not to fret or worry; to know that others have experienced it and Our Lord himself did. All the more then will we pray: "Into thy hands, Lord, I commend my spirit." It is a perfect prayer as I am dying, and a perfect prayer as I live, because it is a prayer of resignation, acceptance, abandonment.

Abandonment to the will of God: That will bring its own freedom because we say deep down, "It doesn't matter what happens; I've abandoned myself to his will. Of course I want to pray that this chalice passes from me, but then I pray, 'Not my will, but thine be done.'"

I accept, Lord, my present situation. I abandon myself to you. I cannot see clearly; I cannot control the future. Lord, I do not know what is happening to me. All the more then will I pray: "Into thy hands I commend my spirit."

It is a prayer of trust. How difficult it is to trust in God. How difficult to say "I leave it to you" and find peace in the saying of it. Trust is an expression of love.

Humility

MOST PEOPLE ARE ONLY TOO AWARE that they have failed to achieve the ideal. Failure, like restlessness, can also be a friend, for its role is to introduce us to humility. Humility is facing up to reality, that is, to the truth about ourselves, our sinfulness and limitations.

Humility is a lovely virtue, edifying to behold, essential to the spiritual life, uncommonly difficult to acquire. It forces us to cast ourselves on the mercy of God. We look now to him to find us, rather than seeing it the other way round. It has dawned on us that our search for him was but our reacting to his for us.

It is often the unlearned and the deprived, as the world would judge, who have the clearest and deepest understanding of the things of God. It will, in fact, be so for those who are truly humble, whether learned or not.

❦

Perhaps a better word than humility is freedom, internal freedom. Freedom from what? From being self-seeking, self-regarding, self-indulgent, self-opinionated. Freedom *for* what? Freedom to find him who is the source of all our desires. Free to love. You cannot love unless you are free.

The consciousness of failure and frailty must not lead to despondency, but rather to complete trust and confidence in God's help. We have to move from pre-occupation with our own perfection to an intense interest in the perfection of God. There is a double process that goes on all the time: Increasingly we identify with that poor tax collector whose prayer was "Lord, be merciful to me, a sinner," while at the same time there grows the conviction that God's love for us is strong, warm and intimate. It is this which calls forth from us a response of love. The abyss of our nothingness has to be filled with the immensity of God's love. Humility is a lovable virtue—delightful to observe in others, painfully difficult to acquire for oneself.

St. Benedict has sometimes been called the Master of Humility. His Rule became, and has always been, a classic on humility. It is a virtue essential to the Christian life. It is fundamental. It is not, as you know, modesty. It is not having a low opinion of yourself—that is not really humility. Humility is facing the truth about who God is, and the truth of "who am I?" St. Benedict makes the first degree of humility the fear of God, that Christian fear of God which does not mean being frightened of God, but is that deep respect, that reverence, that awe, the fundamental attitude of the creature when in the presence of the Creator. The great admission of all that God is, and then the recognition of what we are, which means facing ourselves fairly and squarely and recognizing that I am a wounded creature, that I am part of a fallen race, and all that I have, and all that I can do are in fact gifts which have been given to me by God.

So there is great respect, awe, and reverence for God, and my own lowliness and woundedness put me in the right kind of attitude when I am in the presence of God. But the bond between the greatness of God, and the small, lowly, wounded person that I am is of course that unbounded trust and confidence which was spoken of and written about very eloquently by St. Therese of Lisieux.

Rogues!

What is appealing about rogues—not the wicked or evil person—is their humility. You never meet a conceited rogue!

Peace

PEACE IS SO VERY PRECIOUS, but it begins in the human heart. I speak of that inner peace which is the right ordering of our lives. It comes when we want what is right, and strive to achieve what is good. It is the wanting and the striving that are important.

It is the constant attempt to open up our lives to God, and when he invades the human heart, he establishes peace within his newly won kingdom.

The ideal of peace

In the old Benedictine Breviaries there was a crown of thorns with the words *Pax Inter Spinas*. It has proved to be a marvellous ideal because there are a lot of "thorns" in life, but we have to strive for peace within. So the ideal is peace within your own heart. Realistically it is going to have to be won in order to cope with all the difficulties and problems in life. An ancient definition of peace is tranquillity of order; the opposite is disorder. The Hebrew *shalom* is a state whereby a person or society lives in harmony, in harmony with nature, in harmony with God; the opposite is disharmony, chaos.

There are two words which I believe are the very soul of peace: love and life. Neglect love, neglect life, then you cannot have peace. They find their prototype and highest expression in God himself. God is love; God is life. That is the ultimate explanation as to why these two are so precious and must be respected.

Wouldn't it be good if we lived in a society in which love was respected and honored, and in which life was respected and protected? If we really were concerned for each other, and the needs of the other were more important; if we all thought and acted like that, we would have peace.

Dreams and Visions

We dream of a perfect society in which peace reigns; of a society in which the dignity of every person is respected; where freedom prevails and is responsibly exercised; where duties are as important as rights; where respect and authentic love characterize our relationships, a society in which life itself is honored and treasured. Dreams are normally concerned with the unreal. Visions, on the other hand, are concerned with real possibilities. Can the dreams become visions, and the visions turn into programs of action? I believe so. It is a sad day when a person ceases to be an idealist; a tragic one when a society has lost its vision.

"Your endurance will win you your lives" (Matthew 24:13). Hatred, jealousy, ruthless, and relentless pursuit of power—all these things are part of our society, but I hang on to that Gospel passage. That endurance is not just gritting your teeth and surviving. It comes from the Kingdom of God which is within you. If the Kingdom of God is slow in its realization in the society in which we live, that Kingdom within is happening all the time. So there are qualities which we can have within which give us inner freedom in order to be able to endure whatever the circumstances outside us: an inner freedom which is born of a sense of peace, a sense of joy, a sense of tranquillity.

Those things are gifts which come from God when we begin to want to discover the meaning of love within him. Once you begin to allow that to affect your lives, then peace, tranquillity, and joy begin to take root. Then endurance becomes not just survival, but in fact equips us to make our contribution to bringing the Kingdom of God into the society in which we live.

Though there are tragedies and disasters all around us, none the less we are being called again and again to make our contribution to the values of the Kingdom of God in our society. It is a constant striving that the forces of good should prevail against the forces of evil, but the first battle to be won is always within; to overcome what is not of God within myself in order to enable him to take me over completely and to be an effective instrument.

Trust

MOST OF US LIVE IN A MUDDLE, full of uncertainties and hesitations, with confused ideas about God, often haunted by feelings of guilt. For such, words addressed to God and thoughts about him mean little or nothing. God allows the experience in order to free us from the wrong attachments and draw us to himself. It is good to feel futile before God and wait patiently for him to find us. We may be deprived of the joy of sensing his presence, but we give to him the joy of our trusting him, especially when that trust is given in the dark and without seeking reward. Love of God grows when faith is purified.

In the cell of St. Therese of Lisieux, scratched into the wood she had written: "*Jésus est mon unique amour*—Jesus is my only love." That was not written in exaltation but in near despair. She was thus crying out to her beloved that even when she experienced nothing but absence, emptiness, and darkness, she clung to the assurance of being loved and carried in his arms. That is faith at an heroic level. That is trust, clinging to God when everything in our experience would seem to contradict his very existence, or at least the fact of his love for us.

❦

There are times when the going is not easy. It is as if we were in a storm, and the waves are high. All too often we have the sense of sinking. Life gets on top of us. He, incredibly, remains asleep. We are left to cope as best we can. Then the words, and they betray a little disappointment as he speaks: "Why are you fainthearted, men of little faith?" He wants our trust when trust is hardest to give.

❦

You need to know how not to worry, and to trust God. Most of us have worries, most of us go through periods of darkness, uncertainty, doubt. That is part of living. There was a time when I used to try to get rid of the anxieties and doubts, a time when I used to look for certainty. Then I realized: No, what matters is to trust God. Trusting God means throwing the whole thing into his hands.

❦

It is easy to trust when things go well. It is easy to trust when we see clearly. But it is quite, quite different when we have to walk in the dark and go on trusting. Trusting when things are dark, and accepting when the sword pierces our hearts, these are, in one way, the easiest steps to holiness.

❦

Trusting God when things are not clear is one of the hardest things to do, but one of the greatest marks of our love.

❦

"Into thy hands I commend my spirit." There are times in our lives when it is easy to commend ourselves to our Father in heaven; times when it is easier to give him our trust. But remember that before those words came those other words: "My God, my God, why hast thou forsaken me?" It was in a moment of darkness that he made his ultimate abandonment and total act of trust.

In moments of stress, sorrow, anguish, to be able to pray: "Into thy hands I commend my spirit" is to identify totally with Our Lord in his offering of himself to his Father. In those words lies the secret of holiness. To seek the will of God, to want to do it, accepting the will of God in every circumstance—that is not easy.

"Rejoice, do not be afraid."

"Why should I rejoice?" you might say. It is my life's experience that there is no day on which I shall keep from tears and not know sadness or misfortune. I weep bitter tears for myself when my mind knows only anguish and anxiety, my body pain and fatigue. If God be the goodness which is claimed for him, if he has that love for us which no human love can match, then why does evil seem to rule our hearts and hold sway in his creation? Yet his message is still: "Rejoice, do not be afraid."

Terror comes when we see no escape from the darkness that surrounds us, when we see no light. Terror is the child of despair, ugly, and cruel. But when terror holds us in its grip, hope is often born. Darkness yields to light. A Savior has been born, the Lord Jesus Christ himself, for "God so loved the world as to give his only begotten Son, that whosoever believeth in him may not perish but may have life everlasting." (John 3:16)

Do not be afraid. We need never be alone. Every burden carried by us is also shared by him. He will not always lift the burden from us, but being his too, it is lighter now and easier.

Prayer

"PRAYER IS THE RAISING OF THE MIND and heart to God." That definition in the catechism remains, for my part at any rate, the best of all definitions of prayer. But one word was omitted: trying. Prayer is *trying* to raise our minds and hearts to God.

The only "failure" in prayer is when we neglect it. The only "success" in prayer is the sense of God's presence, or a deep peace and sense of well-being, a marvellous moment of inner freedom. When that comes, it is a special gift from God. We have no claim on it; we cannot demand it. Our part is to turn to him as best we can, trying to raise our minds and hearts to him.

Friendships need space to develop and grow strong. Friends must waste time together. It is also thus in prayer. Prayer is making friends with God, and he with us. Prayer is trying to focus the mind on God, and to admit him into our hearts. Prayer is wasting time with God. Prayer needs space to develop and grow strong.

⚜

Reading and reflecting, either alone or with others, on passages from the Gospel leads to our focusing our minds on Christ, his words and actions. It is the discovering of a friend. It is the beginning of prayer.

We cannot get to God himself except in so far as he enables us to do so. More often than not we get no further than the sense of a presence which is beyond words, images, ideas. It can be likened to being in a room, dark and silent, with a loved one—no words being spoken, no sight vouchsafed, just a sense of the presence of the other. These moments of "presence" are gifts from God, frequent for some, rare for others. Being gifts they are neither of right or reward, but more likely to occur to one faithful in prayer and in life.

⚜

When you get no consolation in prayer, when you feel you are getting nowhere, that may be the best prayer you have ever said, because you are doing it not for your sake, but for God's. Always seek the God of consolation; never seek the consolations of God. It is always that way round.

Quite often we are in a kind of distraught mood, and simply don't know how to pray, feeling that deep sense of being lost. It is good at such times to see oneself rather like the lost sheep in the parable caught in the briars, surrounded by fog; the more you try to escape from the brambles the more you get entangled. The more you try to rush through the fog the more likely you are to get lost. When you are in that mood just wait in your prayer; wait for him to come and disentangle you.

Private prayer

Personal, private prayer: That is when we find ourselves wanting to steal a few minutes out of the day just to be alone with God, trying to give him our attention, trying to focus our thoughts on him, trying to listen when he speaks to us deep within. We are poor, blind, wounded, but those are the best dispositions in order to put ourselves into a situation where we try to raise our minds to think about God and try to purify our desire of him. When I begin to do that, then I am beginning personal prayer. Once I start doing that then my official response—either attending Mass or Evening Prayer—begins to be a little bit different. Public prayer finds its real soul when we start doing seriously private prayer.

Quite often, perhaps even very often, praying words slowly or reflecting on a passage from the Gospel may seem to be frustrating and unrewarding. Do not be surprised or anxious. Such a situation purifies our motive for praying, which is primarily to please God, not to comfort ourselves. Our perseverance is a proof of our love.

The prayer of silence

A very precious way to pray is just through silence. No thoughts or words, just wanting to be silent in the presence of God. Perhaps one of the high points in prayer is where two silences meet: God's silence and our silence. No need for thoughts—and words get in the way.

To be alone with God

Meditation is what we do when we steal moments out of the day to be alone with God, however short that time may be; when we wonder what he is like, when we "explore" God. But we need something to guide us in our exploration. There can be no better starting point than a passage from the Gospel, reading it slowly until it gives up its meaning; then it stirs your heart. When you start to meditate, you will find distractions galore, even boredom, the sense of getting nowhere. The point is you have to stick at it. You have to make an act of faith, because the moments you spend trying to raise your mind to God are precious and golden. There is a kind of paradox in the situation, because the more you try, the more frustrating the activity seems to become. You have to stick at it and recognize the simple truth that if there is any success in prayer, it is a gift from God.

Prayer before a crucifix

I think the crucifix is a great help to prayer. You look and look, and if you are suffering as Jesus did, then that looking will help you understand something about Our Lord, and something about yourself. It gives up its secret. Those are things you cannot write about, things you cannot talk about. Those are things you have to experience. Pray with your eyes in times of stress, no words, no thoughts; just look at the crucifix. Then take out your rosary and kiss the crucifix. That is also true prayer.

Discovering God through experience

Music: There is a Mozart piano concerto which lifts my thoughts right up to God, because I find that piece of music so beautiful that I am drawn to think of the beauty which must exist in God, the origin of all beauty. That beauty experienced reflects something of what it means to be human. Music helps us raise our minds and hearts to God. The prayer of praise comes out of looking at the marvels of creation.

Love: That is a true experience of what God is like. Every experience of human love is an instrument we can use to explore the mystery of God. Friendships, attractions, they all have their part to play and are hints of God saying, "You love that person? You are only drawn to that person because you are drawn to me." All that is lovable has its origin in him who is the most lovable of all.

Woundedness: I've never ceased to wonder at the hurt so many people seem to experience. I've never known a human life in which hurt has not played a part. It must have an important part in God's plan for us: the anguish of losing one we love, all those depressions we can know, the anxieties which can haunt us. The word we often use these days is "brokenness," or that sense of confusion. That can lead to prayer.

When you are very upset, words are impossible, and you conclude prayer is not possible. But in just being in the presence of God with your pain, with your anxiety, what are you doing? You are presenting your wounds to God.

Awareness and desire

Prayer is the effort which we make to have a certain awareness of God which will bring with it a certain desire for him. This desire for God will lead us to seek to have a greater awareness of him.

To some it is the desire for God which comes first and leads to the search. In others it is the search which begins the process and leads to the desire. In fact one feeds the other.

At times it is our admiration for the beautiful, or our desire for the good, or our understanding of the truth, which stirs us to express our joy and our gratitude. At other times it is the suffering which we undergo, or the misery which we feel, which leads us to lay our needs before him.

In either case, whatever may be the individual's religious experience, it is, in fact, always the work of God in the soul, that movement of the Spirit, which makes us cry out, "*Abba*, Father."

Lumen Christi

There is a darkness within each one of us that needs to be dispelled by the light which Christ brings.

There is a darkness in our lives sometimes caused by deliberate and serious sin, sometimes by habit which is displeasing to God.

Sometimes, indeed quite often, that darkness is

not caused by sin or bad habit, but is allowed by God to increase our longing for him, for his light, and for his warmth.

Be still and know that I am God

How difficult it is to make space to be silent and to find solitude to be still. Yet it is in silence and stillness that we hear the voice of God calling to us to look for him in the world he has created, and to listen to his speaking deep within.

To be silent and still is an art to be learned. Be silent and still, and look inwards, first at the darkness within, at conflicting emotions, at the emptiness of the heart, at inner wounds.

We are in need of healing, or nearly always, and in need too of being saved from what is base and ignoble. We are not as we should be. When silent and still, we can, I believe, hear his voice speaking to us through our weakness and inadequacy, coaxing our minds to look for one who will bring order into that inner chaos; but most of all giving forgiveness and encouragement. He speaks, too, through anguish and agony, drawing us away from what separates us from him to look to him for serenity and peace.

There is also light within; our desires and longings, our aspirations to rise above what is of this world, to discover the perfection of love, and a happiness we can never lose. We long to escape from the darkness, that we may dwell forever in the light. Our longing is, ultimately, for what we cannot now have. It will be satisfied only by what is, at present, beyond our reach. Happiness, complete and unending, is for later, not now. Restless hearts will ache no more when in possession of the absolute good.

The Sacred Heart

EVERY AGE PRODUCES ITS particular expression of the Christian truth. Our age produces different manifestations. The Focolare movement, for instance, seems to be in part a reaction to the impersonal character of modern urban society, and is the expression of the desire for inter-personal relationships which come from other quarters, in terms of philosophy. Transcendental meditation is, I think, a reaction to over-verbalized forms of prayer, and corresponds to the need for silence and wholeness within. The Charismatic movement is in part a reaction to the Church's rigid and perhaps over-structured and overloaded system of law: It corresponds to the aspirations people have for freedom and joy of expression in their spiritual lives.

In the seventeenth century the cult of the Sacred Heart was a reaction to Jansenism—that narrowing down of the possibility of salvation which was supposed to characterize the elect. It was a Calvinistic counterpart in the Catholic Church. It is said St. John the Evangelist appeared to St. Gertrude and told her of the significance of the beating of the heart of Jesus which he heard while resting his head on Our Lord's breast—the meaning of which was to be revealed in its fullness when Our Lord appeared to St. Margaret Mary at Paray-le-Monial in June 1675, at a time when the world had grown cold in its appreciation of God's love. Many may not feel attracted to the devotion to the Sacred Heart as presented at the end of the nineteenth century and the beginning of the twentieth, but the theology behind the devotion is of the first importance. We would do well, as a stimulus to prayer, to take the antiphons for Vespers and Lauds.

There are two points I would like to make. First, the Sacred Heart makes divine love human, interprets divine love in human language; for the Word made flesh speaks not only in verbal communication, but also in terms of divine qualities alive in human experience.

May I draw your attention to a quotation from the Gospel? Our Lord had cured the mother of Simon Peter's wife. The sun was going down, and those who had friends afflicted with illness brought them to him, and "he laid his hands upon each one of them" (Luke 4:40): personal, individual attention. We know our Lord's attitude towards a vast number of persons with whom he came into contact, irrespective of their station, their moral probity, whether they were attractive or not. That personal attention reveals in a striking manner what we know is true of

God himself. For each one of us it should be a source of comfort and help: God has this individual concern for me, irrespective of my weaknesses, irrespective of my shortcomings.

Secondly, the feast of the Sacred Heart reveals the vulnerability of God. It is difficult for those who are Thomists to use, of God, the word "vulnerability." How can an unchanging God be vulnerable? It is only in his Son made man that we can get a glimpse of this. Again, one can produce a list of situations in which Our Lord showed his vulnerability: his reaction to the ingratitude of the nine lepers; his weeping over Jerusalem; his grief at the death of Lazarus; his evident affection for Martha and Mary; and his reaction to his betrayal by Judas: "You betray the Son of Man with a kiss?" Read the Gospels again and again, and you will encounter the vulnerability of Our Lord. It seems that God became man to feel what man can feel, to show that he understands. And we can see, since Christ's humanity is part of him and part of the life of the Trinity, how there can be vulnerability in the Trinity itself.

It was to St. Gertrude, so it is said, that St. John talked about the Sacred Heart: St. John, we may say, is the theologian of the Sacred Heart. The Office of the Sacred Heart lays stress on the piercing of Christ's side and the outpouring of water and blood. This was his moment of glory, his hour: The water is a symbol of the Holy Spirit; the blood, the Holy Eucharist. Christians down the ages, contemplating the pierced side of Christ, have witnessed at that moment the birth of the Church. Movements I referred to earlier are movements of which we should be aware if only because they emphasize that it is in the human heart of Christ we find the mystery of God's love.

That is why we observe the Feast of the Sacred Heart. We need to come to the first principles of the spiritual life: the tremendous love God has for each one of us. The consciousness should not only be an inspiration and a consolation to ourselves—it should be a model of our reactions to each other.

Gratitude

To say thank you is very human, and very lovely. Often we show ourselves to be ungrateful or, perhaps more frequently, just by negligence we fail to say thank you. Deep down it is pleasing to be thanked, for it shows we are appreciated, it shows we are loved. On the whole we do not find it easy to thank the people we dislike.

If gratitude is a lovely thing about ourselves, it would be almost unbelievable to think there is not gratitude in God. Of course we will be told that God does not need us. Of course we will be told that everything good comes from him. Of course we will be told that he is in no way dependent on us. It is a nice, precise theology that argues that way.

There is gratitude in God; there must be. What a joy it will be when we realize when we come to the end of our work that deep within us he says: "Thank you for serving me." A glimpse of that truth was given to us by Our Lord himself: "Well done, thou good and faithful servant," congratulations combined with words of thanks.

Mother of God and
Mother of the Church

THERE ARE PERSONS WITH WHOM, from time to time, one comes in contact who have something very special about them—a transparent goodness, such that in their presence we feel inevitably small and unworthy. They are persons before whom we would never say any thing unworthy. Such was the reaction which St. Peter had on one occasion when he fell down on his knees before his Master and said, "Depart from me; I am a sinful man." Quite especially in the presence of Our Lord, that kind of reaction was inevitable. At the same time, in the persons of whom I'm thinking, there is often also a graciousness and consideration which in a second reassures and comforts. So it was with Our Blessed Lord.

There is of course only one person who could in any manner approximate to that nobleness, goodness, and integrity, and that was his own mother. Far beyond and above anything a human could achieve, she, by the grace of God, accomplished a goodness, nobility, and integrity second only to her divine Son. The profound reason for that is her Immaculate

Conception, so that from the moment she began to be, in the womb of her mother St. Ann, she had no contact, no influence, no result of what we call original sin from which she herself was saved. That dignity, nobility, and integrity were the gift of God to her for the function which she was to perform—to be the Mother of Jesus Christ.

That wonderful title—the Mother of God—is one upon which we should often ponder and meditate. Her closeness to Our Lord in life, and her closeness to him now in heaven, should make us confident in the power of her inter cession. She is the Mother of God, Mother of the Church, and so too she is our mother, your mother, and mine, and she should play a special part in the lives of each one of us.

You remember that scene described by St. John when he was standing with her at the foot of the cross and Our Lord said, "Son, behold thy Mother," and to her "Behold thy son." At that moment, as she watched Our Lord dying, she was going through birth pangs again as the Church of God was being born—born through the death and Resurrection of her Son. She became our mother. It would be very wrong if the traditional English devotion to Our Blessed Lady were to become weak or forgotten. I believe that it would be at our peril if we allowed that to happen.

She listened, and pondered in her heart

It is a feminine trait to listen, to receive, to watch. Perhaps that is why more women pray than men. It is the feminine which listens and waits. It is a feminine trait also to see, to observe. The wine has run out. Mary notices, and being a women she has a practical mind. One wonders how intuitive she was. When her Son said words which amounted to "How does this concern you and me?"—implying it was no affair of hers—did she understand he was beginning his public ministry in which for the next two to three years she would have no part? Did it dawn on her that from now on there would be separation, the trial which every mother must face unless she is to ruin her child?

"My hour has not yet come:" the hour when he will pass from death to life and she will again be united with him.

Such then she is: self-controlled, free, noble, sensitive in her capacity to listen, quick to notice the needs of others, generous in her practical help. All that is finest in woman has not been better realized than in her, Mary, who was immaculately conceived. We make a grave mistake in our spiritual lives if she has no part.

The Sound of Gentle Stillness

"GOD IS NOT IN THE HURRICANE, nor in the earth-quake, nor in the fire, but in the sound of stillness;" that, I believe, is the right translation of 1 Kings 19:11,12. My mood is often that of the prophet Elijah. You recall how he sat under a juniper tree and wished he were dead. He had his depressions, identity crises, got discouraged, and sitting under the juniper tree thought he was, like many of us, a square peg in a round hole. Sometimes perhaps Elijah's mood is ours. I suggest that one of the basic prob-lems is discouragement, and the sense that we battle on, day in and day out, and do not always see great results.

We have to withdraw from time to time to be silent and still, to gain perspective, to look beyond this world to search for the origin and purpose of it all. Is there one with power to heal? Is there a teacher who will speak to me of truths my mind cannot dis-cover? Where is the guide to show me the way through life's problems and difficulties? The Christian knows there is such a one. It is he who spoke of himself as the Way, the Truth, and the Life.

The sound of gentle stillness has to be within, and in that context think of yourself coming to the Lord like the blind man in St. Luke (chapter 18): "Lord come to me; be merciful to me a sinner; help me." He stands before you, asking, "What would you have me do?" And you answer, "Lord, that I may see, that I may see with the eyes of faith something of the realities of which you came to speak, something about your presence in the world in which I find myself. Touch my eyes that I may see." I find in that blind man and in the deaf mute good friends, because they reflect what we are like. Those words are addressed to you and me because those characters in the Gospel are us. So in moments of silence we reflect a bit on how much the Word of God means to us, and how much the Sacraments mean to us.

It is in silence that we shall hear a voice deep within us speaking to our nobler selves, calling us to high ideals and generous instincts. Silence is the voice of God, sometimes no louder than a whisper, but speaking to us unmistakably if we learn to listen, to listen to God. That silence, that presence of God, will bring peace to our troubled and divided hearts. It will help to heal and restore our society.

> Come now; turn aside from your daily employment. Escape for a moment from the tumult of your thoughts; put aside your weighty cares. Let your burdensome distractions wait. Free yourself for a while for him. Enter the inner chamber of your soul. Shut out everything except God and that which will help you in seeking him. When you have shut the door, say to him: "I seek your face. Lord my God, teach my heart where and how to seek you." (St. Anselm)

Celebrating the Incarnation—God becoming man—we escape from the tumult of our hearts, and enter the inner chamber of our soul to listen to his Word: The Word calls us from the mist of ignorance and apathy to be silent, to listen to the sound of stillness, and to see in the child born of Mary the Word who became flesh.

Suffering

GOD IS GOOD, LOVING AND ALL-POWERFUL. Then why is there so much suffering in the world, and evil? Why has this young life been afflicted? What is the meaning of this old life so sorely tried and faculties diminished? That young life taken from our midst so unexpectedly and tragically; and we need look no further than to our own personal struggles and the pain we experience. I do not believe that the human mind has ever been able to resolve this great dilemma. I know of no philosopher who has ever given a convincing explanation for the prevalence of evil and suffering.

※

In the end the only explanation my mind has ever found at all adequate is the one provided by the great central Christian truth that God became man, knew the human condition from personal experience (save sin), and so suffered and died. In so doing he gave meaning and value to our suffering and death, with the promise that they lead to something beyond this life, something far better. The meaning of life's sorrows and pains dawns on us only when we look at Our Lord on the cross.

※

From time to time, in our prayers, alone or in community with others, we may be granted the exhilaration of a brief moment on Mount Tabor, and be tempted to build there tabernacles where we can stay forever. But Jesus Christ points the way down the mountain into the world, to tread the lonely path that leads to another hill which is called Calvary, where faith, hope, and love are put to the test.

I am thinking of all those persons who suffer: men and women who suffer in hospitals, prisoners of conscience, those troubled in mind, the anxious, the depressed, the aged, the lonely, the bereaved, the dying. They are evangelists with that special vocation to take up the cross of Christ and follow him. That vocation will be ours at some time or other, in some measure at least. It is always the clarion call to holiness.

※

There are times when any one of us may experience terrible desolation. Then it helps to recall those other days when we caught, albeit "in a glass darkly," a glimpse of him.

Perhaps it was in beauty, seen or heard, or being in the presence of a loved one—an icon of his lovableness. Perhaps we once heard his voice speaking to us in our inmost self and in the inner silence of our soul.

The Mount Tabor experience can, or should, sustain us in the struggle and suffering of Gethsemane and Calvary.

There is in the Church a ministry of healing. There is also in the Church a ministry of suffering, and of all the ministries in the Church it is the most difficult and the most noble. Because in the ministry of suffering you share in the Passion of Christ.

Sickness

To be called to sickness, to be called to suffer, is to be given a special vocation: to carry the cross of Christ. There is always a purpose in suffering, in pain, though very often at the time of our anguish we are unable to see the reason. Conforming to Christ, making up what is wanting in his suffering, helping a sinner to come to repentance, helping a missionary in a far-off land—he uses us for these purposes. That is why the prayers of the sick, and the prayers of the old, are so precious in the life of the Church. Never forget that.

The cures about which we read are not just to demonstrate remarkable and extraordinary powers, but to illustrate, too, the divine concern and compassion for the weakness of man. That sick person is, in some sense, the mirror in which I can see my own frailty. Such thought is depressing only if we fail to listen to those golden words spoken by Our Lord when he was criticized for the company he was keeping: "It is not those who are in health who need the physician but those who are sick." (Matthew 9:12) Those words are addressed to you and to me. Recalled and savored, they enable us to discover again our own need for help.

The cross, our gateway to hope

Persons and nations wander away from God. Pain and suffering, hard to bear, are a call for us to return. So often the cross seems to speak of failure, as was the case with the Master we serve. It seems to speak of failure and disaster, but look long enough at it; its message is clear. It tells us of triumph—in God's way, not ours. So whatever befalls us, we hang on to his words: "God so loved the world that he gave his only Son, so that everyone who believes in him may not be lost, but have eternal life." That truth is our gateway to hope.

Grief

Grief cannot be shared, for it is mine alone. Grief is a dying within me, a great emptiness, a frightening void. It is loneliness, a sickening sorrow at night, on awakening a terrible dread. A reasoned argument explains little for having tried too much.

Silence is the best response to another's grief, not the silence which is a pause in speech, awkward and unwanted, but one that unites heart to heart.

Love, speaking in silence, is the way into the void of another's grief. The best of all loves comes silently, and slowly too, to soften the pain of grief and begin to dispel the sadness.

It is the love of God, warm and true, which will touch the grieving heart and heal it. He looks at the grieving person and has pity, for grief is a great pain. He came among us to learn about grief, and much else too, this Man of Sorrows. He knows. He understands. Grief will yield to peace—in time.

The loss of a loved one is the creation of an emptiness. It is making the space clear which only God can fill.

It is easy to describe the inflicting of physical pain, but it is very difficult to describe what can go on in the depth of the soul of another person, because there can be a depth of sadness which can never be shared by another.

To share suffering with another person can sometimes lighten the burden, but not always. To share it with Our Lord, that is quite different. That is a moment of grace.

Mourning

The tears that dampen our eyes in times of mourning are tears of homesickness, tears of longing for our loved ones. But it is we who are away from home, not they. Death has been for them a doorway to an eternal home. Yet they are with us lovingly and tenderly, waiting for the day when we too will enter the doorway of our eternal home.

No, death is not a separation. It is preparation for eternal union with those we love, in the peace and joy of heaven. When our loved ones die, they do not leave us. They simply begin their eternity.

We need not seek out occasions of mortification or self-denial. The humble and loving acceptance of life's daily burdens, the frustrations of sickness, the darkness of depression or mental distress: these are the Way of the Cross, the Via Dolorosa, which are not our will but God's. They can, and do, lead us into the mystery of God and the joy of new life.

Behind every crucifix

Behind every crucifix, hidden, for we cannot see him, stands our Risen Lord. Hidden in every suffering and pain is the joy of closer union with him. His is the victory. He invites us to share it.

The Sacrifice of the Mass

Every time we celebrate Mass all the suffering and agony of mankind is present. Through that offering, love, forgiveness and hope are in some way being given. Not just to this community round this altar but, like the pebble cast into the pond, the ripples go on and on outwards. So the Mass makes present that one complete Sacrifice of Christ, re-enacted through the consecrated bread and wine—the Body and Blood of Christ—transcending time and space, enabling us to be present at the foot of the cross, and close to the empty tomb. It is our earthly way of being involved in the great heavenly liturgy which is going on all the time.

It is the Church's most precious treasure. It must be ours. The Mass meant so much to the English martyrs; they risked so much just to be present. I feel just a little ashamed when I think how devoted they were. But these great people inspire us to find out more about the Mass, and to love it as they did.

✠

At the heart of that worship (Mass) must be a profound faith in the real presence of Our Lord in the Blessed Sacrament, and, as a result, an attitude of adoration and reverence.

Is not the Mass both sacrifice and communion? And the altar, is that not both the place upon which the sacrifice is offered and the table for the sharing of his Body and Blood? If we forget either aspect, we fall into error.

You cannot live without food; you cannot live without love. Now you see why he gave us himself in the Eucharist. He would not abandon us. He would give us love, give us food. No greater proof of his love for us can there be than the Eucharist. It is a personal gift every time we receive him in Holy Communion.

✠

In a lifetime of attending Mass, or celebrating it as a priest, we shall never, never begin to understand all the riches which are contained in the Mass. Choose a moment in your life where you would like to be, if you had the choice. I would like to think we would choose to stand at the foot of the cross and somehow share his suffering, to be one with him, giving ourselves to our heavenly Father. Whenever we attend Mass we are able to be, so to speak, at the foot of the cross, sharing in his Sacrifice.

If there is another moment where you would choose to be, it might be on that first Easter Sunday, in the Garden with Mary Magdalen. What a joy to see his hands—with the wounds still in them—touching us out of love.

***

I was once invited by a Jewish family to celebrate the Passover with them, and the experience was almost transforming in my understanding of the Mass.

It was at the Paschal meal that Our Lord took bread and changed it into his Body, took wine and changed it into his Blood, so that this meal should commemorate events more important than those concerned with what we call the Exodus. There was a great difference between the two meals. The first merely commemorates past events. The Mass does more. It is a way of bringing into the present what took place on Calvary and at the Resurrection, through the consecrated bread and the consecrated wine: "Do this in memory of me."

***

You and I could not have devised a way of making the Passion, death, and Resurrection present for all men for all time. Only God could devise what he has, in fact, devised; for every time the Mass is said the Sacrifice of Calvary is repeated. Every time you receive Holy Communion the life of the risen Christ is given to you. We witness two things: our gift to God, and the gift of God to us. It is Christ who gives himself to his Father together with ourselves, and it is Christ who is given to us in Holy Communion.

The real presence

God is everywhere, in everything. When you see something beautiful—a sunset, a mountain, a stream—these are reminders of God's presence, revealing his beauty. But when we talk about the real presence, his sacramental presence, that is a very, very important concept. The real presence is the consecrated bread and wine. When I go into a church I always genuflect. Why? Because I believe that in a marvellous way, far beyond our understanding, Christ is truly present in the Tabernacle. If you ask me how this is, then that is theology. But you genuflect because Christ has said it is so. If you try to work out how and why it is, you will never get there. You receive that truth from him. As in friendship, love between two people, you don't work out why you love them—it would kill the spark between you if you analyzed it. But once you love a person, then you grow in the knowledge of them. That is what faith is like, the beginning of a love story. The more you get involved then the more you begin to trust.

A sense of the numinous

How much we should reverence the Mass, and how important it is that it should always be celebrated with dignity and reverence, and in a prayerful manner. That is a crying need for the Church today. We will not do it by making the Mass consciously cheerful, or by eccentric celebrations. We will do it by going deeper into its meaning: That is the secret. We need to rediscover a sense of the numinous. That is what the new generation is looking for.

People come to our churches because they want to discover God, and they want to go out feeling that they have been touched by him. That is so important. It does not mean changing things dramatically, but I do think that restoring respect for the Eucharist and seeking a sense of the numinous are two urgent needs in the contemporary Church.

Devotion to the Blessed Sacrament

We need, in the Church today, to recapture devotion to the real and abiding presence of Christ in the Eucharist. Outside Mass that presence continues and is celebrated through devotion and prayer before the Blessed Sacrament of the Altar. In my view, that devotion was slightly weakened in the years that followed the Second Vatican Council. But we need to rediscover it.

Belief in the reality of Christ's presence in the Blessed Sacrament does not come from reading; it does not come from thinking. It does not come from any person's skill. It comes from faith, from the humility of mind to accept and to say "yes" to what may seem to be unbelievable, namely that the Body and Blood of Christ are present under the appearance of bread and wine.

How important is the precious moment when we receive Our Lord in Holy Communion. It is the moment when we give ourselves to him, as he gives himself to us; a moment when he will speak to us in his own way and encourage us. It is a very personal time and should not be rushed or invaded by distraction. Moments of silence and stillness after Communion are important, moments before the final prayer and blessing, and after, when we stay behind in church—alone with him.

God's Tenderness and Mercy

IN *DIVES MISERICORDIA* THERE is a marvellous foot-note on the Hebrew words for mercy:

> Mercy in God has two aspects, and one word suggests the tremendous faithfulness which God had towards his people, and that fidelity is not only to his people but to God himself. He owes it to himself to be faithful to us.

The other aspect of mercy is best translated by the word "tenderness." I find that concept of tenderness in God absolutely marvellous. It is the feminine in God:

> Can a woman forget her suckling child that she should have no compassion on the son of her womb. Even though these will forget, yet I will not forget you. (Isaiah 49:13)

So that strength which is fidelity and that tender-ness which is love, every time I meet the word mercy in Scripture, *that* is at the back of it.

There is an inspiring sermon of St. Francis de Sales in which he says, "The throne of God's mercy is the misery of man." God could not be merciful—he would almost be denied that quality—if there were not people like you and me to be merciful to. Mercy as defined by St. Francis de Sales was "the greater stooping down to help the lesser." That is a marvellous gesture of consideration: the faithfulness born of tenderness.

The other great revelation of the tenderness and mercy of God is described in Luke (chapter 15): the lost sheep, the lost coin, and the story of the prodigal son. I think that whenever one is depressed about life, or overwhelmed by guilt feelings, if ever one is overcome by a sense of one's own inadequacy, or whenever going through difficult periods, it is good just to go and read quietly and prayerfully Luke chapter 15. It is a marvellous revelation of what we mean to God revealed by Our Lord himself, the highest authority.

It is a bit irresponsible to leave ninety-nine sheep to go after the hundredth. Wouldn't you cut your losses? I would. God does not. But love is irresponsible sometimes. And then, to turn the house upside down just for a coin, as the woman does?

Then there is the story of the prodigal son and that one verse describing the father as he embraces his son: "He kissed him tenderly." You get tears in your eyes when you think of that. The father had been watching out, hoping against hope that he would see his son coming home. He doesn't go after him but waits, hoping, and the moment he sees his son he goes out to embrace him and kisses him tenderly.

That is Our Lord revealing to us what God is like, and that has to be the thought and inspiration of our lives. We have got to allow the thought of his love to become a deep conviction. Remember those words of Our Lord on the cross: "I thirst." It was a physical thirst of course, but also the deeper thirst he had for us.

Forgiveness

"Father forgive them, for they know not what they do." Jesus prayed thus as they drove the nails into his hands and feet. Is there one of us who can claim to be in no need of forgiveness? Not I, at any rate. But do not be distressed, much less despairing. He wants to forgive, even, dare I say it, to find an excuse for our wrongdoing: "They know not what they do." I have but to recognize my need for forgiveness, be sorry for the way I have offended, and be resolved to do my best from now on, and he forgives. He wants to. Lovers do.

In every human life there are things, actions, and attitudes that need forgiveness. There are memories of foolishness and weakness that lurk like dark spectres to haunt us when the spirit is low or the going hard. If only we could hear clearly within us that we have been forgiven. If you and I truly want forgiveness, if our sorrow is real, what is it that stops us from knowing that we have been forgiven? Is it our failure to believe in his love for us? If we turn to him, want to love him, and ask for forgiveness, we may be sure that our sorrow for the wrongs we have done will bring us closer to him and, with that closeness, bring us peace of mind.

Judgement

A priest started his homily at a funeral by saying, "I am going to preach about judgement." There was dismay in the congregation. But he went on: "Judgement is whispering into the ear of a merciful and compassionate God the story of my life which I had never been able to tell." It is a very great encouragement to think of being in the presence of God who is both merciful and full of compassion, because God knows me through and through and understands me far better than I could ever know and understand myself, or anyone else. Only he can truly make sense of my confused and rambling story.

There are times when we honestly do not want to do wrong—that is, to commit sin. But we feel like St. Paul who wrote: "I cannot understand my own behavior. I fail to do the things I want to do, and find myself doing the things I hate." In fact, we find ourselves unable to explain to anyone else, even our dearest friends, our deepest selves with our innermost fears and anxieties. We are frightened that even they will not understand. If only we could whisper into the ear of someone who loves us deeply, understands us completely, and accepts us totally. We go on trying to know God and please him, yet so often we seem to fail, more through weakness than malice.

The time will come for each of us to appear before our God to render an account of our lives. It will not be a frightening moment, unless to the bitter end we have turned away from him or consciously ignored him. Instead it will be a moment of deliverance and peace when we can whisper into his merciful and compassionate ear the story of all our years, and be forgiven and made whole.

Life after Death

IN THE RISEN CHRIST DEATH has lost its hold over mankind. Death for us is not the end of the story. It is the beginning of a new chapter. There is life after death. It is life with God. The purpose of our present life is to prepare for that. Life matters. Human life is of the body and of the spirit; in our present state each depends on the other. Life depends on love; it gives love its real meaning and its purpose. Our Easter faith assures us that life will overcome death, and love will triumph over death.

❧

I think it is very natural for all of us to have a certain fear of death. A lot of people will express it by saying that they are frightened of dying but not frightened of being dead. I think the idea of dying makes people very vulnerable. Also there is a common temptation to question whether there is anything after death. That temptation can come back even after we have experienced a kind of certitude that all is well. I think it often returns to people when they are dying and can be a very considerable trial to them, a very dark tunnel they go through. I have to answer by saying that the human mind is a limited thing; we cannot see beyond this present life.

There is deep within each one of us, normally, the desire to live. We want to hang on to life; we don't want to leave our friends. However difficult life may have been, we want to hold on to it. That is a very deep instinct, and it is my firm belief that through prayer, through reading and reflection, faith teaches us that there is something beyond death, that life is not absurd, that it is not going to end in frustration. It is faith in the person of Jesus Christ who became man, died and rose again from the dead—*that* is the key. When you have got that firmly in your mind and heart, then you can say: "Into Thy hands, Lord, I commend my spirit." That prayer, which I pray daily, is the prayer of Our Lord himself when he was dying on the cross. It is a prayer of complete trust in God.

The life of the soul

The life of the soul, both now and hereafter, is one of knowing and loving. In this it reflects the very nature of God himself. One day we shall see God as he really is, face to face, know him immediately without any intermediary. Beatitude, that is perfect happiness, will follow from that vision and we shall be in that endless now of ecstatic love, as we are united to him who is absolute truth and goodness and, as such, infinitely lovable. For us it is not so yet. At present our knowledge of him is imperfect and needs must be mediated through finite things and persons; either through his creation or through the sacred words which convey to us his divine message.

❧

"I am going to prepare a place for you." Yes, there is a place ready for us, a new beginning for which life has been but a preparation, a place where God will wipe away every tear, and death will be no more. A place where loved ones will be seen again, a place where all our noblest desires will be totally satisfied, for we shall see God as he truly is. We shall discover that all that we thought and experienced about love were but hints of the real thing when we are together, at one with God.

Looking forward

The greatest grace which God can give is the knowledge that he loves each one of us more than any lover ever loved his, or her, beloved. To realize that, and to allow it to sink deep into our minds and hearts, can change our lives completely. Who can separate us from that love?

As we approach the last bit of the journey, there are days when we fear that we face an unknown, unpredictable, uncertain future. That is a common experience. But do not worry, because the time comes when we no longer carry heavy bags and all those possessions. We shall travel through the cold, grey light of a bleak English morning into God's spring and summer, into his light and warmth.

✥

"This day you will be with me in paradise" (Luke 23:43). This day will inevitably come for each one of us; we do not know when. But it most surely will come, and what a joy it will be when we hear the words: "This day you will be with me in paradise." We must move in our spiritual lives from thinking of death as the great enemy and begin to think about "this day" as the one when we shall be going home, the one for which we were made, and for which the whole of our lives is the preparation.

Life is indeed a pilgrimage as we walk each day closer towards its end, which is the vision of God. We are made for that, and life is a preparation for the moment when we move from this situation into eternal happiness.

Joy and sorrow, agony and ecstasy, pain and well-being: they walk hand in hand up that hill which is called Calvary. But beyond it is a place where there is no more death, no sin, no pain, only empty tombs and life everlasting.

The moment of ecstasy

I see this life as a period of training, a time of preparation, during which we learn the art of loving God and our neighbor, which is the heart of the Gospel message; sometimes succeeding, sometimes failing. As we learn, then many things begin to look different. Death, for instance, comes to be seen as the way which leads us to the vision of God, the moment when we shall see him as he really is, and find our total fulfilment in love's final choice. The ultimate union with that which is most lovable, union with God. I call that the moment of ecstasy.

The One who will understand,
who will forgive,
who will console.
That is my view of God.